M000218993

Guided Journal

A LITTLE BIT OF

AURAS

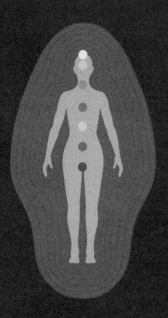

Guided Journal

A LITTLE BIT OF
AURAS

YOUR PERSONAL PATH TO
ENERGY AND WELLNESS

CASSANDRA EASON

STERLING ETHOS
New York

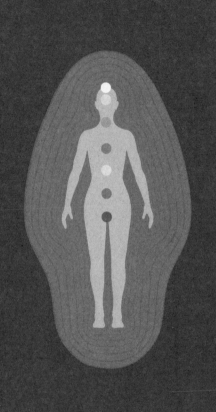

THIS BOOK BELONGS TO

_____

_____

_____

STERLING ETHOS
New York

An Imprint of Sterling Publishing Co., Inc.
1166 Avenue of the Americas
New York, NY 10036

Portions of this publication previously published as *A Little Bit of Auras*.

ISBN 978-1-4549-4031-9

Distributed in Canada by Sterling Publishing Co., Inc.
c/o Canadian Manda Group, 664 Annette Street
Toronto, Ontario M6S 2C8, Canada
Distributed in the United Kingdom by GMC Distribution Services
Castle Place, 166 High Street, Lewes, East Sussex BN7 1XU, England
Distributed in Australia by NewSouth Books
University of New South Wales, Sydney, NSW 2052, Australia

For information about custom editions, special sales, and premium and corporate purchases,
please contact Sterling Special Sales at 800-805-5489 or specialsales@sterlingpublishing.com.

Manufactured in Singapore

2 4 6 8 10 9 7 5 3 1

sterlingpublishing.com

Cover design by Elizabeth Mihaltse Lindy
Interior design by Sharon Jacobs

Image Credits
Fuzzimo.com: cover; Shutterstock: DeoSum: cover, throughout;
satit_srihin: cover, throughout; solarus: cover

❧ CONTENTS ☙

INTRODUCTION

Picture the glow surrounding young lovers, or a child enchanted by a magical Santa grotto. The glittering grotto might be decorated with tinseled fairies. Saints, like those in traditional paintings, are portrayed with their heads surrounded by a golden sphere. People may say if someone makes them angry, "I saw red" or "She was green with envy" because that is the main color being radiated and picked up intuitively without being physically seen. Auras like these are part of our natural perception of the world. In early societies, hunters looking out from a cave high in the hills would know if distant approaching tribesmen had friendly intentions by the energies they emitted.

We all have an aura, a rainbow-colored energy field, usually invisible to the physical eye, which can be perceived psychically with remarkably little practice. Our aura surrounds our whole body in a three-dimensional ellipse, made up of seven different-colored bands. This aura reveals our mood, our personality, and the status of our health. Our aura may guide our interactions with others, even though our actions may run counter to outward logical signs. Yet, invariably our aura-prompted actions are startlingly accurate.

At its most radiant and strong, the aura can reach outward to an extended arm span around the body. This spiritual bioenergetic aura field varies in size and density under different conditions. Gautama Buddha, the spiritual leader on whose teachings Buddhism was founded, was said to have an aura that extended over a range of several miles and therefore influenced people throughout that area.

THIS JOURNAL

You will learn about your aura and the auras of the people around you with the information in this book. It can be used on its own, or in conjunction with *A Little Bit of Auras*, which includes more in-depth information on some of the material in this book.

❖ 1 ❖

INTERPRETING THE AURAS OF OTHERS

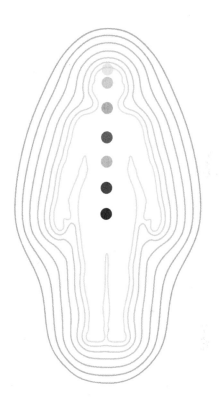

I N PRACTICE, ONCE YOU HAVE STARTED TO LEARN
about aura color significance, you will suddenly become aware
of one or two predominant colors around people. You will also
spontaneously become aware of someone's mood, even if you see
him approaching across a parking lot, by the colors you see or sense
around him, especially around his head and shoulders.

THE SEVEN MAIN COLORS OF THE AURA

Red, orange, yellow, and green represent the inner earthly daily living and relationship aura levels, while blue, indigo, and violet reflect the higher spiritual levels. White is often seen as part of or suffusing the seventh layer.

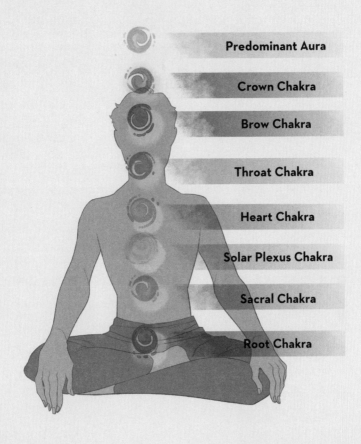

Predominant Aura

Crown Chakra

Brow Chakra

Throat Chakra

Heart Chakra

Solar Plexus Chakra

Sacral Chakra

Root Chakra

RED

For action, survival, change, power, physical energy, courage, determination, and passion; the color of the crusader.

Red forms the innermost aura layer.

POSITIVE QUALITIES As clear bright red, scarlet, or rich ruby, it indicates vibrant life, the ability to overcome any obstacles, a desire to initiate positive change, and a passionate lover.

NEGATIVE QUALITIES Bright metallic red signals a short temper, a bullying nature, a tendency to erupt if frustrated, and impulsivity or risk taking. When the red is dull or harsh, it reveals suppressed fury, an irritable nature, and resentment over perceived injustices, which build up rapidly. Scarlet-flashing auras suggest a flirtatious nature and maybe inappropriate passion.

ARCHANGEL Camael, archangel of Mars, who rides his leopard to victory

FRAGRANCES Cinnamon, cypress, dragon's blood, ginger, and mint

STRENGTHENING GEMS AND CRYSTALS Blood agate, fire opal, heliotrope, garnet, jasper, meteorite, obsidian, red aventurine, red tigereye, and ruby

CHAKRA Root or base

ORANGE

For confidence, independence, and a strong sense of identity, fertility, self-esteem, health, happiness, and personal desires; the color of the integrator.

Orange is the second layer of the aura, moving out from the body.

POSITIVE QUALITIES Warm, rich orange indicates the ability to integrate different aspects of life; sociability; self-motivation, originality, and creative abilities; and an open-minded, enthusiastic, and optimistic nature. Bright orange is an excellent sign for anyone wanting children.

NEGATIVE QUALITIES A pale orange may indicate a lack or loss of identity or low self-esteem, someone who bases his sense of worth and identity only on what others think, or someone who is being bullied. Murky orange may indicate an oversensitive ego and territorial tendencies. Overly harsh orange represents excesses and obsessions, especially issues relating to food and self-image.

ARCHANGEL Gabriel, archangel of the moon

FRAGRANCES Eucalyptus, jasmine, lemon, and myrrh

STRENGTHENING GEMS AND CRYSTALS Silver, moonstone, mother-of-pearl, pearl, opal, and selenite

CHAKRA Sacral

YELLOW

For logic and intellectual achievement, speculative abilities, versatility and mental dexterity, and changeability or restlessness. The color of the communicator and the traveler.

Yellow forms the third level of the aura, moving outward, and is one of the everyday living layers.

POSITIVE QUALITIES Clear lemon yellow is the color of a focused mind and a sharp memory, of financial and business acumen, especially in speculation and technological expertise. Bright yellow is a color of joy and of clear communication, and brilliant canary yellow suggests a potential actor or entertainer. Clear yellowy brown augurs a scientific or mathematical mind.

NEGATIVE QUALITIES Irregular harsh streaks of yellow indicate hyperactivity, while mustard yellow may mask jealousy or resentment. A metallic yellow haze conceals less-than-honest intent and a tendency toward gambling. Sharp lemon yellow may be logical but may also represent a sharp, sarcastic tongue. Mustard yellow may also indicate spite, or a potential gossip. A very cold yellow may suggest that the head always rules the heart.

ARCHANGEL Raphael, archangel of healing, travel, and the entrepreneur

FRAGRANCES Lavender, lily of the valley, melissa (lemon balm), lemongrass, and fennel

STRENGTHENING GEMS AND CRYSTALS Calcite (yellow and honey calcite), chrysoberyl, lemon chrysoprase, citrine, jasper, rutilated quartz, and yellow topaz

CHAKRA Solar plexus

GREEN

For love, fidelity, trust, harmony, natural growth in every way, and concern of the environment; the color of the child of nature.

Green is the fourth layer of the aura, moving outward, and the last daily life level. At its outer limits, it reflects love of humanity.

POSITIVE QUALITIES Rich, clear green reveals a trustworthy, loving heart, who is generous with time, love, and money, and whose words come from the heart. A green aura is the sign of a person deeply committed in love. Emerald green shows a natural healer, especially in the alternative field, and someone who is naturally lucky.

NEGATIVE QUALITIES Pale green suggests emotional dependency. A dull, muddy green can reveal conflicting emotions or a potential emotional vampire who sucks energy from others. Yellowy green can be a sign of possessiveness and emotional blackmail. Lime green may imply stress in current relationships. A cloudy or dark green aura may indicate those who love unwisely and too much, or who are pining for unrequited love.

ARCHANGEL Anael, the archangel of lasting love, fidelity, and natural growth in any matter

FRAGRANCES Apple blossom, lemon verbena, magnolia, and vanilla

STRENGTHENING GEMS AND CRYSTALS Amazonite, aventurine, chrysoprase, emerald, fluorite, jade, malachite, moss agate, peridot, and tourmaline

CHAKRA Heart

BLUE

For ideals; broad vision, both of perspective and physical horizons; natural authority; and healing powers transmitted through higher sources; the color of the seeker of truth.

Blue is the first of the higher and outer aura levels and the fifth one, moving outward from the body.

POSITIVE QUALITIES Royal blue indicates an integrated personality, with a keen sense of justice and natural powers of leadership. Bright blue is very creative and also altruistic. Pale blue is the color of the idealist with global vision. Clear blue represents objectivity, and the possessor is often a gifted speaker and teacher. Blue auras suffusing other aura colors can be seen around spiritual healers; authors; and musicians, actors, and other performers.

NEGATIVE QUALITIES Dull, dense blue may represent increased conservatism and a concern for rigid rule keeping, regardless of circumstances. Harsh blue is a sign of someone who is autocratic, opinionated, and intolerant of others' lifestyles and beliefs.

ARCHANGEL Sachiel, archangel of the harvest, truth, justice, prosperity, expansion in every way, and traditional learning

FRAGRANCES Fennel, honeysuckle, lotus, sage and sagebrush, and sandalwood

STRENGTHENING GEMS AND CRYSTALS Aqua aura, angelite, blue chalcedony, blue lace agate, blue quartz, celestite, cobalt aura, kyanite, iolite, lapis lazuli, sapphire, topaz, and turquoise

CHAKRA Throat

INDIGO

For inner vision and psychic awareness, spirituality, and knowledge of the future and of past lives/worlds; the color of the seer, the wise one, and the evolving soul.

Indigo forms the second of the higher levels of the aura and is the sixth layer, moving outward from the body. It often merges with the violet outermost layer.

POSITIVE QUALITIES Clear indigo indicates acute sensitivity to people's unspoken intentions and awareness of the spiritual world, enhanced intuition, clairvoyance (psychic vision with the inner eye) and clairaudience (psychic hearing), and charitable care for all in need. The brighter shades indicate a fertile imagination. Deep indigo is present in the auras of wise older people. Lavender, which is a shade related to indigo, brings sensitivity to the higher powers within nature, and those with a lavender tinge in their aura enjoy an awareness of devas and a gift for herbalism.

NEGATIVE QUALITIES When the indigo aura is blurred, it implies that its owner is spending too long on daydreams and illusions or on self-pity and a tendency to stress,

especially absorbing other people's negative moods.
A dark indigo indicates isolation and disillusionment with
the world. An all-suffusing indigo can reveal a person with
Asperger's syndrome or other conditions associated with
oversensitivity to the world, especially among the young.

ARCHANGEL Cassiel, archangel of consolation and
compassion for the world's sorrows, who turns sorrow to joy
and brings acceptance of what cannot be changed

FRAGRANCES Mimosa, myrrh, mugwort, patchouli,
and violet

STRENGTHENING GEMS AND CRYSTALS Amethyst,
ametrine, fluorite, kunzite, sodalite, super seven, and
tanzanite

CHAKRA Brow or third eye

VIOLET

For medium senses and connection with other dimensions and with ancestors, angels, and spirit guides; the color of the mystic, the visionary, and of integration between all aspects of the self and with the spiritual world.

Violet is the highest aura level and merges into white and gold, as it is joined to pure cosmic energies. White, especially, often forms part of this aura layer.

POSITIVE QUALITIES A connection with unconscious wisdom and the collective knowledge of humankind in all places and ages. The ability to think laterally and globally and to disregard immediate gain to achieve a long-term goal; a love and tolerance of humanity with all its weaknesses and a peacemaker with the highest ethics; the ability to heal through higher energy sources, such as angels and wise guides; a tendency to gain recognition, especially in the performing or creative arts, in a meaningful rather than a merely commercial way.

NEGATIVE QUALITIES When violet is too pale, drive, incentive, and stamina may be lacking, and grand plans rarely come to fruition. Too harsh a violet indicates perfectionism and/or an unrealistic idea of what is possible—that is, the inability to accept everyday life and people with all their imperfections. A dull violet may indicate depression.

ARCHANGEL Zadkiel, angel of truth and justice, higher healing and abundance, the performing arts, and all alternative therapies and major charitable initiatives

FRAGRANCES Bergamot, magnolia, lilies, orchids, and sweetgrass

STRENGTHENING GEMS AND CRYSTALS Charoite, lepidolite, purpurite, purple spinel, sugilite, titanium aura, and violan

CHAKRA Crown

WHITE: The Predominant Higher-Aura Color

For limitless potential, boundless energy, the free-flowing life force, the color of the soaring spirit, the quester, and the innovator.

White often forms part of the outermost seventh aura layer in highly evolved people, especially where indigo and violet merge in the sixth aura layer, or white may overlay the violet. Indeed, from the sixth layer on, the colors become much more blended.

POSITIVE QUALITIES At its most vibrant, this aura is the color of those who follow a unique life path and make a difference in the world. It draws pure, undiffused light from the cosmos that can be used for healing. It is a highly evolved color, indicating higher levels of consciousness, purity of intention, and the quest for what is of worth.

NEGATIVE QUALITIES A pale, misty white may suggest a person who is out of touch with the real world and is involved in grandiose spiritual plans that have no foundation in reality. Murky white masks feelings of alienation and an unwillingness to reach out to others. An overly brilliant white heralds a holier-than-thou attitude and obsession with physical perfection and beauty; also, the drive to push ahead, regardless of the consequences to others, and eventual burnout.

ARCHANGELS Michael, the archangel of the sun, and Gabriel, the archangel of the moon, for the synthesis of outer and inner worlds. The two archangels represent the synthesis of male and female energies. Michael has a male focus, and Gabriel has a female focus.

FRAGRANCES Chamomile, copal, frankincense, and sunflowers

STRENGTHENING GEMS AND CRYSTALS Clear aragonite, diamond, clear fluorite, clear crystal quartz, herkimer diamond, opal aura, rainbow quartz, white sapphire, white topaz, and zircon

Use this space to reflect on the colors of the aura and what they mean to you. Which colors resonate with you? Which colors do you feel that you'll sense in friends and family?

_____

_____

_____

_____

_____

_____

_____

_____

_____

_____

_____

_____

_____

_____

_____

_____

_____

_____

THE SEVEN AURA BANDS, AND HOW TO IDENTIFY THEM

The seven bands appear as a rainbow halo around the body in the shape of an ellipse, but, again, they form most clearly around the head and shoulders.

Ask your psychic vision to show all seven strands to you. Relax and look through half-closed eyes, if necessary slowly closing and opening your eyes two or three times as you look at yourself in a mirror, or around the head and shoulders of the person you are going to help.

These seven color bands, and the subsidiary colors within them, hold the key to health and well-being, and through them you can cleanse and energize the whole aura. You can also heal and strengthen individual aspects of it that cause the body, mind, and soul to be out of balance.

If the aura becomes blocked, overactive, or weakened, the effects may eventually bring on conditions to which a person has a predisposition, or they may exacerbate existing physical problems. For example, stress is often reflected in the aura as jaggedness or tangles and it can eventually create illnesses or encourage existing ones.

With their permission, you can cleanse, heal, and empower the auras of friends and family or clients. If it is someone who is ill, ask if he or she would welcome a healing. It will be accepted if it is meant to be.

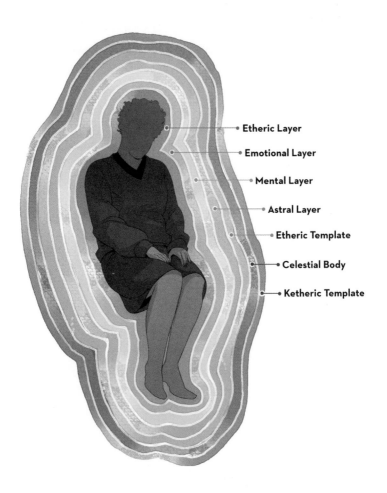

• Etheric Layer

• Emotional Layer

• Mental Layer

• Astral Layer

• Etheric Template

• Celestial Body

• Ketheric Template

The Seven Aura Layers

Each aura layer is empowered by and, in turn, empowers our chakras, the invisible energy centers within our body. Each aura layer reflects the color of its chakra. The effects of blocked or overactive chakras are reflected in the aura layers and can be healed or strengthened by working directly with the aura. The aura colors spill out from the inner spiritual body of which the chakras are a part.

1. THE ETHERIC LAYER: THE INNERMOST LAYER OF THE AURA

This first aura layer is powered by the red base, or root chakra energy center. Brown, black, and gray aura colors emanate from this chakra.

This red aura layer reflects your basic instincts and your overall physical health. It encompasses your flight-or-fight mechanisms, together with the physical stamina that energizes the body. Uncontrolled anger and aggression, and its more positive side—keen awareness of opportunity and danger, and survival mechanisms—reside here.

The etheric aura layer, like the base or root chakra, rules the legs, feet, and skeleton. This includes the teeth, joints, muscles, the cell structure, the bowels, the prostate, the circulatory system, and the large intestine.

2. THE EMOTIONAL LAYER: THE SECOND LAYER OF THE AURA

The second layer of the aura is powered by the orange sacral chakra. The aura at this level appears as light orange or silver, especially when sexual or fertility matters figure prominently in a person's life.

This is the layer of the aura that deals with desires—whether for love, sex, approval, food or other oral stimulation, such as coffee or cigarettes, and eating disorders. Here also dwell our basic intuitions or gut feeling, as it is sometimes called.

The emotional aura layer, like the sacral chakra, rules water within the body—and so issues with fluid retention and hydration—hormones, the reproductive system, the kidneys, fertility, and the bladder. It is a layer especially sensitive to stress.

3. THE MENTAL LAYER: THE THIRD LAYER OF THE AURA

The third layer of the aura is powered by the golden-yellow solar plexus chakra.

This is the layer of the aura that reflects our personal power, confidence, determination, and our unique self. It is often in overdrive in our 24/7 modern, competitive world.

The mental layer and the solar plexus chakra rule digestion, the liver, the spleen, the gallbladder, the abdomen, the stomach, the pancreas, the small intestine, metabolism, the lower back, and the autonomic nervous system.

Work with yourself and anyone with whom you have regular contact, studying their rainbow bands. Record your observations of their auras in the fields on the following pages.

4. THE ASTRAL LAYER: THE FOURTH LAYER OF THE AURA

The fourth layer of the aura is powered by the rich green heart chakra. Sometimes pink emanates from this aura as well.

This aura level controls the ability to give and receive love, and to understand and empathize with others without drowning in guilt or assuming too much responsibility.

Turquoise, as a slender outer band within this aura strand, is prominent if a person is highly spiritually aware and altruistic.

The astral layer and the heart chakra rule the heart, the chest and breasts, the lungs, the lymph glands, blood pressure and circulation, the upper back, and the skin. It also controls viruses and allergies.

5. THE ETHERIC TEMPLATE: THE FIFTH LAYER OF THE AURA

The fifth layer of the aura is powered by the sky-blue throat chakra.

This is the layer of the aura concerned with creativity, communication, and listening, as well as speaking, formulating and expressing ideas, and developing ideals. Implicated on the autism spectrum, this layer of the aura also controls dreaming.

The etheric template and the throat chakra rule the throat and speech organs, the thyroid gland, the neck and shoulders, the passages that run up to the ears, and the mouth and jaw.

6. THE CELESTIAL BODY: THE SIXTH LAYER OF THE AURA

The sixth layer of the aura is ruled by the indigo third eye or brow chakra.

At this aura level, which deals with imagination, inspiration, nightmares, fears, and phobias, your spiritual well-being can affect your physical well-being.

The celestial body and brow chakra control the eyes, the sinuses, the ears, headaches (including migraines), the pituitary gland, the cerebellum, and the forebrain, and their influence radiates into the central cavity of the brain.

7. THE KETHERIC TEMPLATE OR CAUSAL BODY: THE SEVENTH LAYER OF THE AURA

The seventh layer of the aura is powered by the crown chakra, whose color is violet, merging into pure white and gold. This is the aura level of total integration of your physical, emotional, psychological, and spiritual self.

The ketheric template and the crown chakra rule the skull, the autoimmune system, all neurological functions, the upper brain, the cerebral cortex, the cerebrum, the central nervous system, hair growth, and the pineal gland. They integrate the functioning of the body, mind, and spirit.

Work with yourself and anyone with whom you have regular contact, studying their rainbow bands. Record your observations of their auras in the fields on the following pages.

DATE   TIME

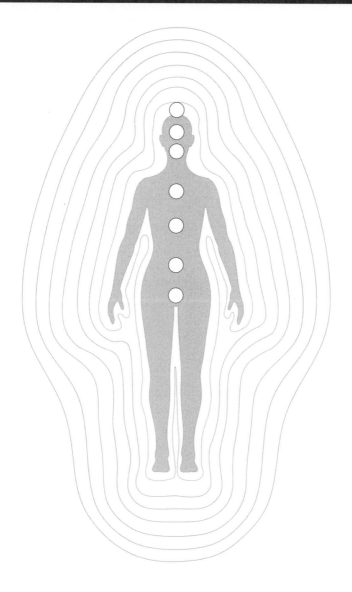

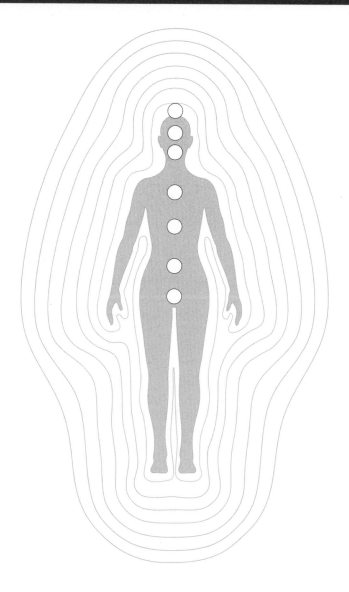

DATE TIME

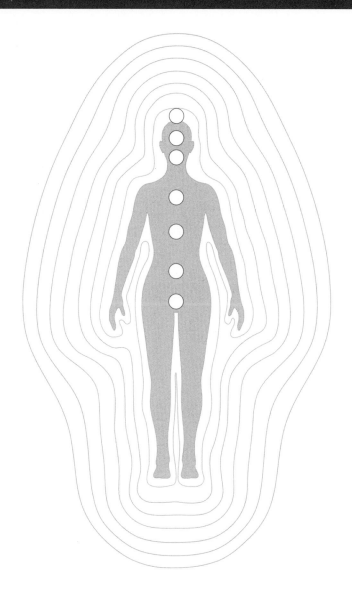

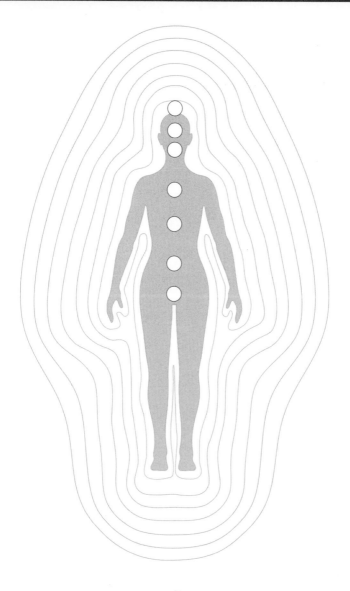

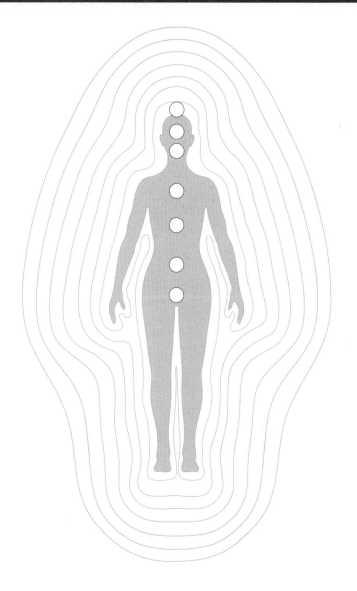

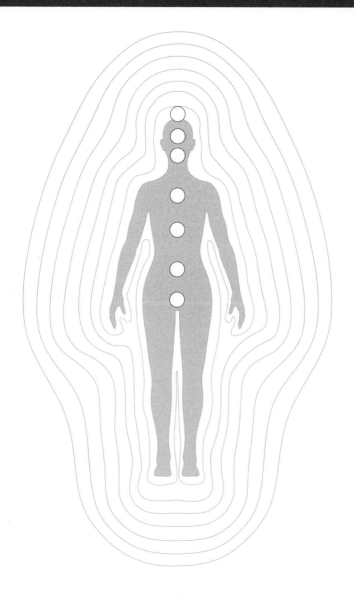

DATE   TIME

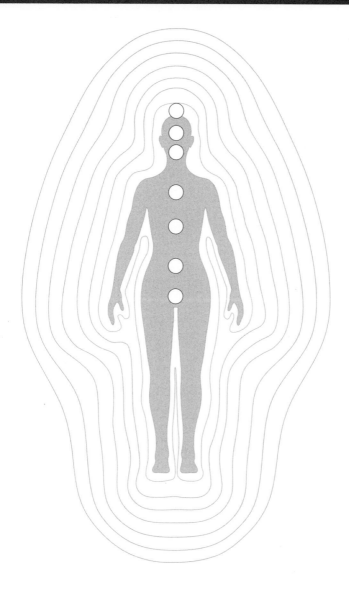

SOME QUESTIONS TO ASK YOURSELF
AS YOU INTERPRET AURAS

- Is one layer of the rainbow unusually predominant, whether it is extra bright or dull, and are there any special situations that seem to cause this band to stand out? If you can monitor and record over a short period and in different environments or with different people present, you will see a pattern emerging and either encourage or intervene in the situation.

- Alternatively, does one rainbow band permanently stand out, perhaps indicating a part of your life or that of a loved one that is evolving or important to develop? Is there one that is very pale, cloudy, or missing? Again, note if this varies according to other people who are present—for example, a very pale orange band if you or someone you know feels intimidated by a dominant personality. If any band colors are missing, go back to the aura health suggestions and see how you can increase use of one or two techniques to restore aura balance to the rainbow.

- Do the personality aura color(s) reflect as predominant bands in the seven rainbow colors?

- Health and well-being can also be reflected in the rainbow bands. If you monitor your own bands of color and those with whom you have a loving connection, the colors form a good early warning system. For example, the indigo band may become a dark, dull color or streaked with jagged silver if a migraine or headache is potentially hovering, even a day or so before. Time to take remedial action or slow down if you are on a major 24/7 dash.

- Is there an additional band not currently in the personality aura that is consistently bright? This could indicate personality traits that, with encouragement, may be ready to emerge. If so, note this and, if positive, explore ways you can develop this.

- If a personality aura in someone you know seems to be changing over a period of a few months, detect if there is a major life change approaching, anticipated or feared. This might be developing a particular talent professionally, changing profession, falling in love, moving in with a partner, planning a baby, or relocating overseas. These can show in the seven bands even before they occur in actual daily life.

- If the band affected looks dark or is wavering, ask yourself or the person whose aura you are studying if they have any worries or fears about a planned change or are being blocked from going forward. The best aura readers tend to be the best counselors to friends, family and colleagues, because intuition is, in both cases, the key to sensitive understanding. The rainbow bands can give you advance knowledge to ask the right questions.

Monitor the seven aura bands in yourself and anyone whom you see regularly to become aware of their underlying concerns, but do talk and listen, don't just jump to conclusions. For example, if the green band of your partner seems pale or dull, this doesn't mean they are falling out of love with you, merely that work may be taking more energy than usual. This would show in a harsher blue or lemon-yellow band, so make time for fun together. Your seven bands are like a piano and sometimes need subtle retuning with practical action.

If your own rainbow is looking persistently dull or overly harsh, carry a set of rainbow crystals with you and sleep with them around your bed to restore balance. If one area is deficient of color, add an extra crystal in that color or burn the same colored candles as you relax.

Alternatively, go back to the tips in the next section of this book and see if lack of time has let some of them slip. Note any that will be especially helpful and can be done quickly and easily.

IMPROVING THE HEALTH OF YOUR AURA

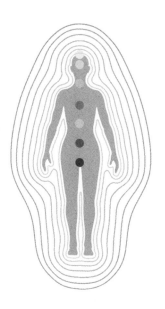

TWENTY WAYS TO
INSTANTLY IMPROVE YOUR AURA

1. **EAT BRIGHTLY COLORED** fruits and vegetables, either raw or lightly cooked, to make your aura more radiant. Berries and raw peppers are instant aura energy lifters.

2. **GO OUTDOORS** in natural light for a few minutes whenever possible if you work in a setting of constant artificial lighting, which is an aura drainer.

3. **WORK WITH A DISH OF MIXED CRYSTALS** in the different colors of the rainbow. When you wake up, pick one crystal without looking and hold it in your cupped hands. We are automatically drawn through the sensitive energy centers in our palms and fingertips to the most helpful crystal and this will be the color your aura needs most.

4. **IF YOU FEEL HOSTILITY AROUND YOU,** move the palms of your hands together and outward again so they almost touch and then a few inches (several cm) apart, very slowly to build up the energy between them. When you feel your hands becoming heavy, move your hands quickly apart (it may be hard) and shake your fingers over your head and shoulders from above your hairline. This will create psychic sparks around your whole aura that will deter spite or hostility.

5. **KEEP A POT OF GROWING FRAGRANT FLOWERS** around your home or office to circulate the life in order to infuse your aura with energy and health.

6. **ON DARK, COLD DAYS,** wear at least one bright color to stimulate your aura and counteract the sleepy, dull energies that can sap enthusiasm.

7. **MAKE DRINKS WITH WATER** in which you have soaked a blue lace agate, jade, or amethyst crystal for two or three hours, and offer it to critical or overactive people. It will blend their auras into harmony with yours. If it isn't possible for them to drink it, then drinking the water yourself will protect your aura against them.

8. **DRINK PLENTY OF WATER EVERY DAY.** Coffee, tea, and carbonated drinks with additives can make the aura energy field dry and irritable.

9. **GENTLE EXERCISES,** such as dancing, swimming, walking, or cycling, will help to circulate your aura energies even better than overly vigorous activities that may deplete reserves by causing energies to shoot out randomly in all directions.

10. **AVOID EXCESSIVE CONTACT** with synthetic materials and, whenever possible, wear natural fabrics next to the skin to avoid stifling your aura.

11. **IF YOU WORK WITH HIGH-TECH** machinery or use a mobile phone or computer at home a lot, set green malachite or gray smoky quartz between you and the machine. Alternatively, keep a small crystal with your mobile phone to prevent it from sucking energy from your aura.

12. **PETS ARE VERY GOOD** at transferring their loving, accepting energies from their aura to yours. As you stroke your pet, picture his soft brown, pink, and green energies overlaying your own like a gentle protective cover.

13. **SEND AURA POWER** to anyone in need, such as a child or a partner, even if she is absent, by holding a picture of her and, as you gently breathe, imagine a soft pink light enveloping her. This is good if the loved one is far away.

14. **KEEP POTS OF FRESH HERBS GROWING** in your kitchen to spread a sense of abundance and to draw good things into the aura or energy field of your home.

15. **PLACE WIND CHIMES,** bells, feathery plants, and mirrors around your home to keep the aura of the home lively and health-giving energies flowing.

16. **GOLD JEWELRY** will fill your aura with confidence and focus, and is good if you need to impress others or show authority.

17. **SILVER JEWELRY** will increase harmony and bring peace and reconciliation to any interaction.

18. **COPPER JEWELRY** fills your aura with love and will attract and increase love in your life.

19. **IF YOU FEEL TOTALLY EXHAUSTED** or depressed, gently pass a clear quartz crystal pendulum or point in clockwise circles through your hair, then down over your eyebrows in clockwise circles, just touching the skin, then over your throat and your wrist points for your heart energies. This will give you a rapid infusion of power and enthusiasm.

20. **WHEN YOU NEED TO SLEEP OR REST,** pass either an amethyst crystal pendulum or a crystal point counterclockwise in the same way mentioned in step 19 to still your aura so you can rest and be restored.

As you implement these changes, keep ongoing notes of your progress, both where the steps to improving your aura health are easy and where they will need extra input. You will find that some of these suggestions already automatically fit into your daily life. Others will bring beneficial changes, a new awareness of your own increasing energies and free-flowing feelings and the way you impact on others, after you have tried them a few times.

What has worked instantly for you?

_____

_____

_____

_____

_____

_____

_____

_____

_____

_____

_____

_____

What are some examples of where you have noticed increasingly effective improvements, heightened energy levels, and harmony in yourself?

How has this made professional and social interactions flow much more smoothly?

_____

_____

_____

_____

_____

_____

_____

_____

_____

_____

_____

_____

_____

_____

_____

_____

_____

If you have a family, partner, or friends with whom you share a home, have you noticed that you become less affected by unintentional tactless words or careless actions of others and more ready to listen and explain calmly what you are feeling?

Note any new positive interactions as a result of the aura work you are doing, especially with people you consider difficult, as you radiate your newfound calm or confidence. If you hit resistance, try extra aura health tactics.

Which of your aura health activities can you share with family and friends or introduce to daily practice in the workplace? Aura health spreads like ripples in a pool.

Have people visiting you or with whom you work and socialize commented how well you are looking, or have they asked if you have had your home redecorated?

_____

_____

_____

_____

_____

_____

What have they said?

_____

_____

_____

_____

_____

_____

_____

Are pets calmer and appear more ready for fun?

Use the space below to write about any changes that you have noted.

_____

_____

_____

_____

_____

_____

_____

_____

What is the most beneficial aura health step you have taken, and how can you build on this to improve other areas of aura health that need more input?

_____

_____

_____

_____

_____

_____

_____

_____

How have you made your workspace more harmonious and focused as a result of applying some of these ideas? Crystals and plants are instant and ongoing mood lifters, for example.

_____

_____

_____

_____

_____

_____

_____

_____

_____

_____

_____

_____

_____

_____

_____

_____

_____

_____

Finally write anything in the list that doesn't seem to work, and you can perhaps try again in a few weeks.

✦ 3 ✦

MOOD AURA

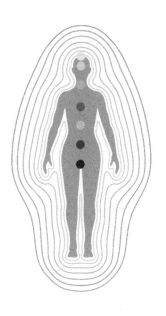

HUMAN AURAS ARE CONSTANTLY CHANGING. Our auras are affected both positively and negatively by the energy fields of other people with whom we interact and the physical, mental, and emotional environment in which we live and work. These mood auras can also be influenced by memories of past situations and fears or anticipation about the future.

Some people are prone to rapid mood swings and are especially sensitive to external events and inner thoughts. The auras of hyperactive and ADHD children, or those with Asperger's syndrome, are wide open and therefore are easily affected by unfriendly peers and insensitive adults. Others on the autistic spectrum have closed their auras at a very early age to avoid the intense pain of interactions with the world in general—the good as well as the bad.

Being able to instantly read the mood auras of individuals and, with practice, groups of people at work or in social situations tell you what is going on, even under the surface, and puts you one step ahead.

Throughout the day, situations and people may not only temporarily affect your aura color, but if you feel strongly or are concentrating hard, one mood color will flood the whole aura. For example, if you were fully concentrating on learning something new, a clear yellow would predominate. If you were working on your spiritual development, one of the higher aura bands, such as indigo, would temporarily suffuse the seven aura bands, even for a while covering the ever-present stable personality or permanent aura I will describe in the next chapter.

These temporary colors tend to flicker and be quite transient and, when you first learn to read the aura, the mood will usually be the first and clearest color you see, since it is fueled by emotion and so easily spreads throughout the whole energy field.

This has been the case time and time again when I have worked with people, interpreting the images created by an aura camera. An aura camera converts the predominant aura colors into a printed image of a head-and-shoulders view. It works when an individual places his hands on metal plates as he sits in front of the aura camera.

If one color predominates in the photograph, it will be because that color reflects the immediate strong mood being felt by the person and so blots out most or all of the other colors. For example, I watched a couple having an argument while standing near an aura camera, because the man said the photo would be a waste of money. His partner snapped back, saying he was mean and always stopped her from having fun. The woman was still fuming when she sat for her picture, and refused to calm down before having it taken. As a result, the photograph displayed a harsh red color all over the aura, spilling out to the edges of the picture. Her partner had stormed off, so, regrettably, I could not see his aura picture.

What would you have expected his mood color to be?

IDENTIFYING THE MOOD AURA

When you see this aura, it will be quite sparkly. You will probably initially see the mood aura color in your mind. If you are very logical, your mind may initially block even this process. In this case, say or write the first color that comes into your mind as you look at the person, for that invariably reflects her correct mood aura.

Begin by programming your psychic eye and intuitive senses by saying aloud or in your mind that you first wish to focus on the mood aura.

Look either directly toward the subject or, if it would be impolite to stare if she is close, somewhere over her left or right shoulder, whichever is easier. You might even look at her from the back view, as the aura extends all around the body for an arm span or more at its brightest. The head and shoulders give you the clearest view.

Slowly close your eyes and just as slowly open them and blink.

You should instantly see the mood aura.

Whether you see the colors in your mind or externally, the mood texture will be slightly more ethereal than the physical body.

The mood texture will resemble finely woven, colored, sparkly, net curtain material, moving quite fast all the time, like shallow water rippling over sand or sunlight dancing on water.

If the mood aura fades before you have processed the information, repeat the exercise and the second time the mood aura color should remain visually or in your mind for a longer time.

The mood aura may increase or decrease in size and intensity, even within less than a minute.

Your psychic sensing or claircognizant abilities (also called the sixth sense or, by Scottish people, kenning) will kick in quite early.

If the mood aura is pale or, conversely, very harsh, you may sense sudden exhaustion and defeat in your own body, perhaps because the person whose aura you're reading is being bullied by a colleague or partner, or you may feel a grating in your teeth, like biting on ice, if the person you are studying is about to shout down someone else.

If a child consistently comes home from school with a pale mood aura, make tactful inquiries if he or she is being teased, even if you see no outward signs of physical harm.

Remember, a mood need not be caused by a present event; sometimes an old memory can intrude and flood us with sorrow or joy.

Given practice, you will intuitively sense the time frame of the event causing the mood color, whether current, recalled, anticipated, or feared. This intuitive interpretation is possible because all impressions, images, and words spoken are stored in our aura, including anger, passion, memories, and future fears. As you learn more about the aura, you will be able to accurately pinpoint these moods and apply the necessary remedy to counteract any negativity.

If you yourself have seemingly inexplicable mood changes, see if you can link the timing of those changes to a similar situation in the past. If the mood is not positive, once you know the cause of the mood, in yourself or in others, you can then take action to say the right thing, offer support, steer clear of the trigger of discomfort, or work with an antidote color.

Start work as an aura detective, especially when you notice a couple or family members' auras affected by each other's mood, to detect trouble brewing.

How can you intervene tactfully using your own aura positivity to defuse a situation that might impact on others?

_____

_____

_____

_____

_____

_____

_____

_____

_____

_____

_____

In time you'll be able to sense underlying feelings and mood interactions, even if two people are smiling or saying nice things. Before long, a seemingly throwaway remark or negative body language gesture will reveal the true picture. Sometimes, too, even if two people in the office or at a party are outwardly not communicating, you'll see the frisson of feeling and sometimes even more between them in neon or brilliant glowing scarlet colors or rich green love mood aura vibes.

Note down date, time, a few lines on the background, and if or how the auras changed during the interaction.

DATE   TIME

INTERACTION

_____

_____

_____

_____

_____

AURA BEFORE INTERACTION

_____

_____

_____

_____

AURA AFTER INTERACTION

_____

_____

_____

_____

_____

_____

_____

DATE   TIME

INTERACTION

_____

_____

_____

_____

_____

AURA BEFORE INTERACTION

_____

_____

_____

_____

_____

AURA AFTER INTERACTION

_____

_____

_____

_____

_____

_____

_____

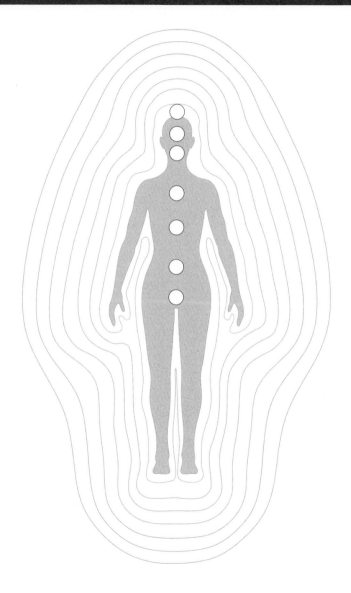

DATE   TIME

INTERACTION

_____

_____

_____

_____

_____

AURA BEFORE INTERACTION

_____

_____

_____

_____

_____

AURA AFTER INTERACTION

_____

_____

_____

_____

_____

_____

_____

DATE   TIME

INTERACTION

AURA BEFORE INTERACTION

AURA AFTER INTERACTION

DATE   TIME

INTERACTION
_____
_____
_____
_____
_____
_____

AURA BEFORE INTERACTION
_____
_____
_____
_____
_____

AURA AFTER INTERACTION
_____
_____
_____
_____
_____
_____
_____

DATE _____ TIME _____

INTERACTION _____

_____

_____

_____

_____

_____

AURA BEFORE INTERACTION _____

_____

_____

_____

_____

AURA AFTER INTERACTION _____

_____

_____

_____

_____

_____

_____

_____

DATE _____ TIME _____

INTERACTION _____

_____

_____

_____

_____

AURA BEFORE INTERACTION _____

_____

_____

_____

_____

AURA AFTER INTERACTION _____

_____

_____

_____

_____

_____

_____

DATE   TIME

INTERACTION

AURA BEFORE INTERACTION

AURA AFTER INTERACTION

DATE   TIME

INTERACTION

_____

_____

_____

_____

_____

AURA BEFORE INTERACTION

_____

_____

_____

_____

_____

AURA AFTER INTERACTION

_____

_____

_____

_____

_____

_____

_____

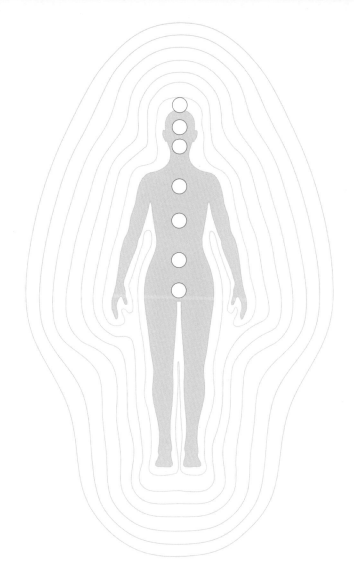

Stop and take time to frequently tune in to the current mood aura of those whom you are emotionally close to or share workspace with. You can do this when you see them approaching, even as you look at them through the window crossing the car park or walking up the path. Tune especially into the feelings you subsequently get when they are talking to you that flow from the aura—cold, anxious, irritable—and be aware that is their aura, not yours, expressing this.

Your partner or a colleague may be fuming or worrying about something that happened before you spoke to them. It is too easy to take their mood personally and fuel an unnecessary confrontation.

Note times when you were aware of this and with careful questioning, you can trace the origin of the mood aura to a bad commute or a nasty memo they weren't revealing when snarling at you.

Mood auras can be strongly sensed telepathically even if you can't always see them. Trust what you feel and as you keep notes you will discover your first impressions were right.

Note the times before you were able to consciously read mood auras when you felt guilty or got swept up in someone else's mood, and how you would now change the interaction.

DATE   TIME

INTERACTION

MOOD AURA DESCRIPTION

MOOD AURA ORIGIN

WHAT DID I FEEL

WHAT CHANGED

DATE   TIME

INTERACTION

MOOD AURA DESCRIPTION

MOOD AURA ORIGIN

WHAT DID I FEEL

WHAT CHANGED

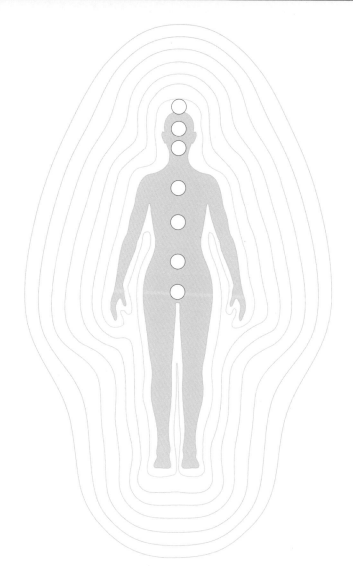

DATE   TIME

INTERACTION

MOOD AURA DESCRIPTION

MOOD AURA ORIGIN

WHAT DID I FEEL

WHAT CHANGED

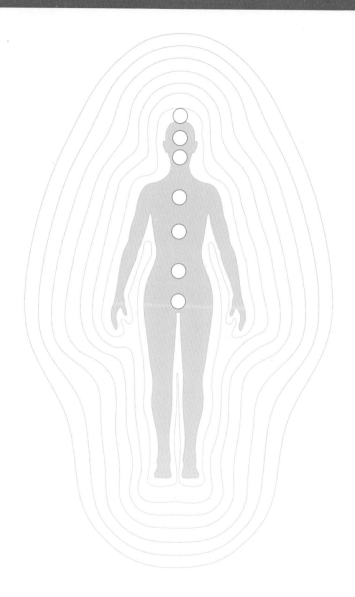

DATE   TIME

INTERACTION

_____

_____

MOOD AURA DESCRIPTION

_____

_____

MOOD AURA ORIGIN

_____

_____

WHAT DID I FEEL

_____

_____

WHAT CHANGED

_____

_____

_____

_____

_____

_____

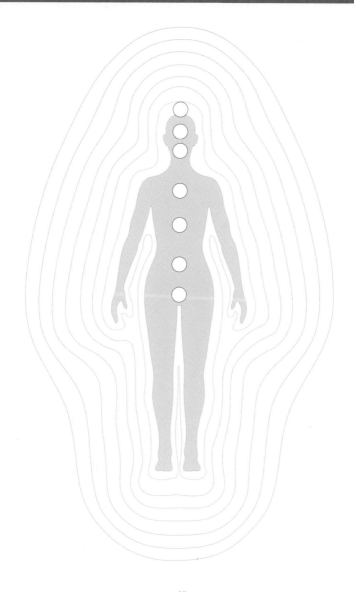

DATE   TIME

INTERACTION

_____

_____

MOOD AURA DESCRIPTION

_____

_____

MOOD AURA ORIGIN

_____

_____

WHAT DID I FEEL

_____

_____

WHAT CHANGED

_____

_____

_____

_____

_____

_____

_____

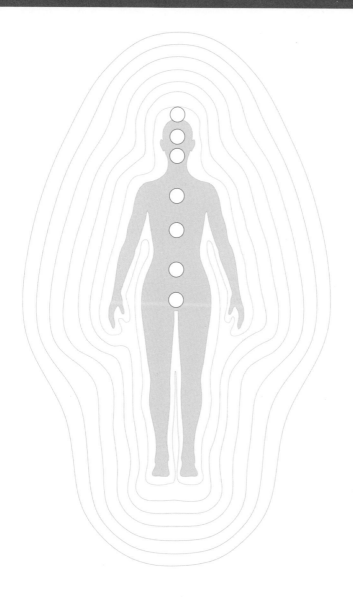

DATE   TIME

INTERACTION

MOOD AURA DESCRIPTION

MOOD AURA ORIGIN

WHAT DID I FEEL

WHAT CHANGED

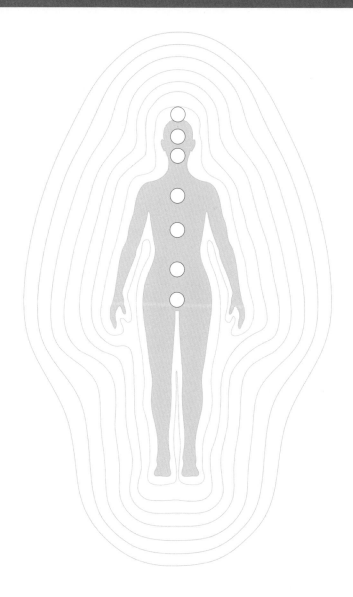

What are triggers in your life that can affect your own mood?

Record them so you can counter them as, or even before, they occur.

DATE	TIME	

4

PERSONALITY AURA

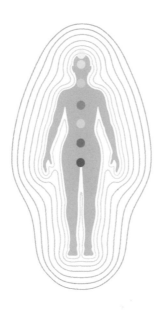

THE PERSONALITY AURA HELPS YOU UNDER-
stand what makes people tick. It gives insight into the kind
of people they are and the things that matter to them. As
a result, you'll figure out the right approach to take in dealing with
them. You may have already noticed one, two, or occasionally three
areas of matte color behind the flickering mood aura. Personality
auras are more static and smoother. In babyhood through early child-
hood, the personality aura changes rapidly. During the teen years
and the early twenties, you can also see speedy changes in the personality aura, though the core color will remain the same or only
slightly modified.

In adulthood, alteration in personality aura colors is brought about by major life-changing events. So, for example, falling deeply in love (emerald green), giving birth to a child (pink), and studying or having a gift for spirituality (indigo) will cause dramatic alteration in a relatively short time. By contrast, being deeply hurt by a betrayal in love can, almost overnight, put up dark or harsh color barriers.

IDENTIFYING THE ASPECTS OF THE AURA YOU MOST NEED

In Chapter 3, we concentrated solely on the mood aura. Now the more permanent personality aura will fill your focus. Think of it as changing lenses on an expensive camera to focus on what you need to capture most.

Eventually, you will spontaneously sense or see all seven aura colors to read auras for personal information, rather than to heal. You will focus on mood and personality predominantly and bring these into sharper focus.

If you want to see the personality aura directly after you have studied the mood, wait a few moments, close your eyes, and rest all your psychic senses by picturing a deep blue velvet cloth in your mind.

The mood aura will automatically recede and, as you open your eyes, the personality aura color(s) will slowly replace the mood aura colors in your psychic vision. We'll probe the techniques for seeing or sensing the personality aura strands later in this chapter.

THE IMPORTANCE OF UNDERSTANDING THE PERSONALITY AURA

As you increasingly trust your findings, you may sometimes discover a surprising mismatch, such as a person who does not seem to enjoy her job no matter how good she is at it. As an example, you may find an indigo accountant or a lemon-yellow child-care worker, who, later in life, changed their career, from one they originally adopted to please parents or because it seemed like the sensible option. If you work as a therapist or in human resources, personality aura reading is a valuable skill to understand dilemmas that have no apparent cause. However, that indigo accountant may be very intuitive, knowing instantly where issues or mistakes lie, and is popular with clients because of a gentle encouraging manner. The child-care worker might also be excellent at organization and seeing that every child is safely cared for.

When going on interviews, you can quickly understand not only the mood of the interviewers but the core values that they consider important. Whether you're out at a singles event, meeting colleagues at a new job or a training course, going to a social event with a partner, or meeting a partner's family for the first time, you instantly become aware of the right approach and topics that are safe to broach.

In time, you will be able to read personality auras by voice, by speaking on the telephone, or even by viewing online dating photographs.

STUDYING THE PERSONALITY AURA IN DETAIL

Those who have just one color in their personality aura tend to be very definite, fixed characters, whose opinions are not easily shaken.

However, if the personality aura is a pale, faded color, the person may have been emotionally or physically abused at some point in his life and has withdrawn from expressing opinions or even likes and dislikes.

Techniques to See the Personality Aura

Work initially with subjects you know well until you feel confident in your aura-reading skills. Then try reading the personality auras of strangers or acquaintances who come into work or whom you see socially, perhaps at the gym, so you can gain some feedback from tactful questioning about their lifestyle and preferences.

As with studying the mood aura, program your psychic eye by asking it to show you the personality aura, and that alone.

Look toward your subject, but this time do not stare.

Gaze through half-closed eyes and the softer, smooth matte personality aura may spontaneously appear. If not, close your eyes as slowly as possible and open them just as slowly, but do not blink. The personality aura should remain present for a minute or two, or even longer. If not, repeat closing your eyes and opening them slowly and smoothly. You may, as you become more experienced, be aware of the mood aura in the background flickering behind the personality aura.

As with the mood aura, if you cannot see anything internally or externally, name or write down the color(s) you sense without pausing. This will cut through any unconscious blocks.

Recording the Personality Aura

When you record your findings in your seven-band diagram, color and label the diagram according to what you see and the relative positions of the colors, as a new personality aspect may be emerging.

In all likelihood, the personality aura color(s) will fill most or all the seven bands. However, sometimes the personality aura only covers the outer layers of the diagram, or each remains within its own related color strand. If this happens, especially if these color strands are not next to each other, it may be that the personality is being suppressed by circumstance or denying the true self. This can be confirmed if, for example, there is pale green in the fourth naturally green heart band moving outward, which suggests the person is living through others.

The relative positions of the colors are significant in assessing the predominant nature of the person, as one color may totally obscure the other(s). Alternatively, there may be a thin band of a subsidiary color farther out toward the cosmos, indicating it has not yet been awakened, but could hold the key to happiness.

The closer a personality color is to the head or crown chakra, the more it manifests in daily life. And if you see evenly sized bands, that person is going to be balanced in different aspects of her personality, perhaps logic and creativity or work and home interests.

If the personality of the person is especially dominant, the personality aura color(s) may spill over the bands into the space around the bands. This is often true of single personality aura colors, such as the autocratic, rigid, dark blue.

Have a good selection of pencils, crayons, or marker pens on hand. Choose a set that has at least three shades that are widely available for each color.

For new people in your life, whom you will see regularly, make studying their personality auras an ongoing exercise. When you're out and about, note on your smartphone, or even scribble on the back of an old memo or printout, the personality colors you see. You can then, when you have uninterrupted time with these significant people, add to or confirm instances that back up or modify your initial impressions.

As you see these key people more, whether socially or professionally, note if their personality aura is generally unchanging and predominant or often totally obscured by the current mood aura.

Orderly people tend to have an orderly aura. Emotional or empathic folk have powerful mood auras that can temporarily but regularly mask or override the personality aura.

Plan strategies for people whose personality auras are predominant regardless of mood and also for the changeable-mood-aura folk, so you're not caught off guard. Occasionally you'll find that someone's mood colors are almost always the same color as their personality aura. Such people are either very much in harmony with themselves or, alternatively, have strong brakes on emotions.

Study also people to whom you are emotionally close but may not see very often. Does any subsidiary personality color predominate in different situations, for example the successful logical yellow businesswoman or man displaying soft green in their personality aura when spending the long summer vacation with their grandchildren? They may define themselves in both roles depending on the environment.

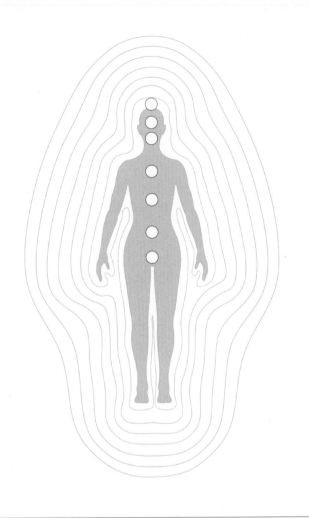

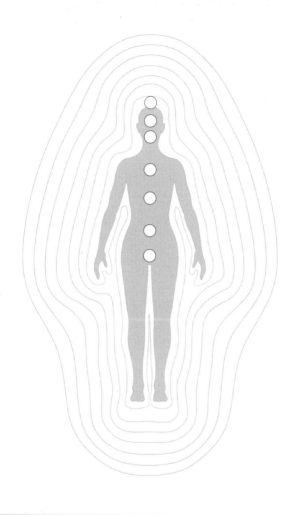

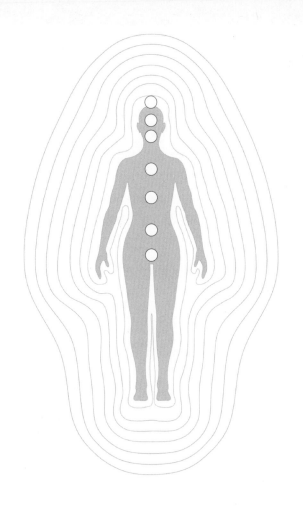

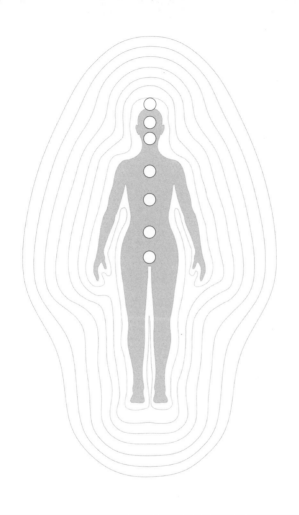

DATE **TIME**

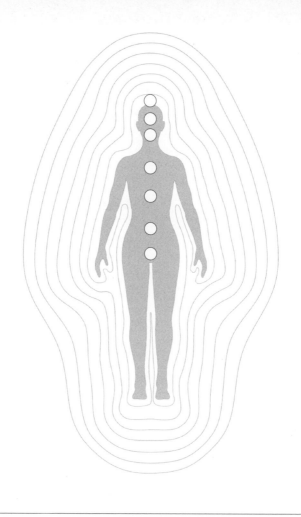

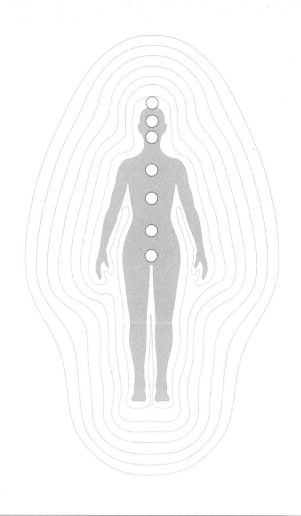

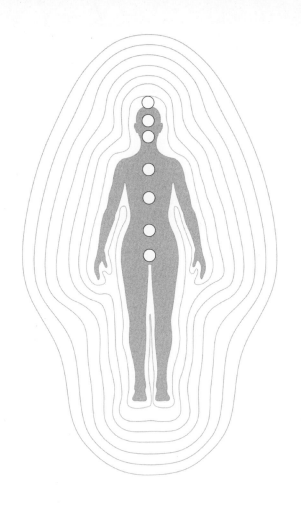

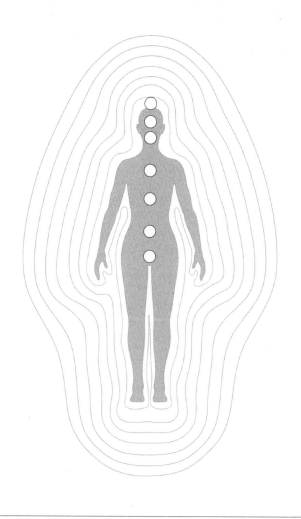

_____

_____

_____

_____

_____

DATE   TIME

Think about your interactions with others. Are you attracted to people with certain personality auras or personality aura combinations? Maybe they seem to appear by chance in different areas of your life. Take a head count in different parts of your life if this seems to be so, and work out why this is, whether they are an opposite and you feel stimulated by this, or they are like yourself and you feel comfortable with like-minded people.

Is there a particular personality aura that provokes clashes with you?

_____

_____

_____

_____

_____

Why?

_____

_____

_____

_____

_____

❈ 5 ❈

AURAS IN THE HOME & WORKPLACE

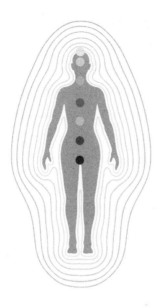

AURAS REVEAL HIDDEN INFORMATION AS WE interact with neighbors, friends, family members, and colleagues—both in the workplace and at any social gathering.

By studying these aura connections, you can almost instantly grasp the dynamics of any situation, avoiding the pitfalls and seeing possibilities for creating positive links, even with difficult people.

HOW TO STUDY AURA INTERACTIONS

The auras of individual family members, and people in the workplace or at social gatherings, are constantly interacting, whether positively or negatively. They may try to dominate and manipulate (watch out for murky yellows and greens), or they may merge, like a constantly flowing sea, to create a harmonious, collective aura in the home or workplace.

It is easy to read aura interactions. Lines can come from anywhere in the sender's aura but are usually perceived emanating from around the sender's brow, between and just above the eyes. They are received in the same place.

TUNING IN TO AURA INTERACTIONS

Relax, half-closing your eyes, allowing your eyes to go into soft focus as you people-watch in a connected group, whether extended family, an office setting, a seminar, or a larger gathering, such as a wedding or a graduation.

Look for interconnecting lines and shades of color moving between people, noting people who have no lines connecting with them or who send out a lot of them, but don't receive connections back. Also watch for people who receive a lot of attention, but don't respond emotionally. Even within the lines, be aware of dark knots or overly harsh shades.

Love aura rays are always strong, but are they a possessive pea green or pale green, indicating unrequited love, or is there a two-way, rich, green energy?

WORKING WITH AURAS IN FAMILY, WORKPLACE, AND SOCIAL INTERACTIONS

Connecting rays are usually mood aura links. However, the mood aura may be influenced by the underlying personality aura in terms of suppressed personality clashes or strong compatibilities. Intense compatibility happens in love, where, if lovers are standing close to each other, both their auras may seem to merge.

If family and social gatherings or workplace meetings cause conflict, plotting aura interactions can help you understand the underlying dynamics, avoid pitfalls, and find out who is generating the difficulty. The person you thought was a sweet old aunt, the office mouse, or a longstanding gym member furiously pumping iron in the corner might actually be the ones slyly stirring the pot.

Study group auras everywhere—nights out with friends, a family dinner at home, at a wedding, when meeting new family members, when you're starting a new job, or wherever new people gather. What people say and even their body language, which can be controlled, do not necessarily reflect what is going on inside.

Write notes on your phone in situ to remind yourself of what you perceive. At a party, scribble your observations on the back of a napkin.

Afterward, plot the group dynamics at the celebration or other gathering on the following pages.

DRAWING GROUPS AND DYNAMIC AURAS

1. **DRAW AND NAME CIRCLES REPRESENTING EACH** character you observed closely, and use colored pencils or very fine marker brushes in a variety of shades to draw the interconnecting rays and plot the connections.

2. **DRAW THE RAYS GOING TO EACH OF THE PEOPLE** from an individual as a single line and those coming back toward them as a separate line, with arrows on each to indicate the direction the rays are traveling. For rays falling short of the intended recipient, place a vertical line at the end.

3. **ONCE YOU HAVE DRAWN THE RAYS BETWEEN** everybody, your figure will resemble a spider web. Who has the most rays going toward them? Who is sending out the most, trying to be the life and soul of the party? Are the people in the family or social gathering communicating and, if so, are they expressing themselves in positive ways and with positive intent? Note the shades and you'll discover if anyone is totally isolated by choice, sending out repelling rays.

4. **NOTICE AURAS WITH HOOKED LINES, LIKE TENTACLES,** that are manipulative or possessive. Conversely, observe sociable rays, reaching out like rays of the sun everywhere. Some rays may be closed and compact or misty and secretive, even though the person may appear outgoing in their words and actions.

5. **FOLLOW THE LINE TO WHERE IT ENDS,** or the person nearest to where it ends, if it stops short and disperses.

6. **PLOT OUT THE GROUP DYNAMICS AND WRITE DOWN** your observations on the blank pages that follow.

GROUP DYNAMICS

NOTES

INTERACTION   DATE

_____

_____

_____

_____

_____

_____

_____

_____

_____

_____

_____

_____

_____

_____

_____

_____

_____

_____

GROUP DYNAMICS

_____

_____

NOTES

_____

GROUP DYNAMICS

NOTES

INTERACTION
DATE

GROUP DYNAMICS

NOTES

INTERACTION   DATE

GROUP DYNAMICS

NOTES

GROUP DYNAMICS

NOTES

GROUP DYNAMICS

NOTES

INTERACTION _____ DATE _____

_____

_____

_____

_____

_____

_____

_____

_____

_____

_____

_____

_____

_____

_____

_____

_____

GROUP DYNAMICS _____

_____

_____

NOTES _____

_____

GROUP DYNAMICS

NOTES

GROUP DYNAMICS

NOTES

Aura study should be a very busy area for your notes. It is one where you are regularly monitoring aura interactions, so it's worth looking back over what you have previously written about similar social occasions.

For example, if you have a particular family event coming up or projects to organize in the workplace, check the interactions between certain people, positive as well as negative, that you recorded at a past gathering. Rearrange seating plans accordingly. Use strong confident aura people to act as foils between an over-dominant and shy sensitive aura person. At work, mix leaders and followers, those who can see the whole picture with others who are good at details and the fine print.

If it is a new event or meeting or this is the first time you have studied aura interactions, try, if possible, to read before the event the mood and personality auras of those you know will be present.

Write down possible good aura mixes in advance as well as ones that you know won't work. A few minutes making notes before an event will be more than repaid in a harmonious and productive occasion.

If you identify a troublemaker, see if you can keep them busy with tasks that will harness their skills to avoid mischief-making.

When organizing official events, committee meetings, or social evenings, be alert, especially if the people aren't that well known to you, of knots, hooks, or over-bright colors appearing between auras. Is there someone, even though standing in the center of a group, who is totally isolated? Have one or two deputies who can, with a tactful word from you, step in to regroup people or find a welcoming aura to embrace your isolate.

Try initially to scribble down notes or a diagram on your smartphone, or even on a napkin, about any immediate clashes you see looming.

If trouble is brewing, you may notice a thick sludge-like aura over a particular corner, so send some sunny-aura folk over.

The result of organizing aura interaction is that everyone will compliment you on how well the meeting or social occasion went and will go away happy.

Beforehand, if you can, set either calming pink and blue crystals or candles around, or if you want a stimulating fun atmosphere, lots of orange and yellow.

NAME_____ DATE_____

INTERACTION_____

REASON FOR INTERACTION_____

_____

_____

OBSERVATIONS_____

_____

_____

NAME   DATE

INTERACTION

REASON FOR INTERACTION

OBSERVATIONS

NAME _____ DATE _____

INTERACTION _____

REASON FOR INTERACTION _____

_____

_____

_____

OBSERVATIONS _____

_____

_____

NAME _____ DATE _____

INTERACTION _____

REASON FOR INTERACTION _____

_____

_____

_____

OBSERVATIONS _____

_____

_____

INTERACTION

REASON FOR INTERACTION

OBSERVATIONS

NAME _____ DATE _____

INTERACTION _____

REASON FOR INTERACTION _____

_____

_____

OBSERVATIONS _____

_____

_____

INTERACTION

REASON FOR INTERACTION

OBSERVATIONS

NAME _____ DATE _____

INTERACTION _____

REASON FOR INTERACTION _____

_____

_____

_____

OBSERVATIONS _____

_____

_____

INTERACTION

REASON FOR INTERACTION

OBSERVATIONS

❖ 6 ❖

SEALING YOUR AURA

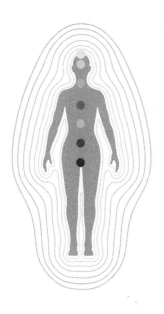

SEALING YOUR AURA AFTER CLEANSING AND empowering it allows positive energies to enter your aura and filters out negativity and undue stress from daily life. Over time, negativity and stress can undermine your health and well-being.

SEALING THE AURA WITH LIGHT

Sit or stand with your hands about 2–3 inches (5–8 cm) apart, palms vertical and facing each other.

Move your palms together so they almost touch, then move them slowly outwards 2–3 inches (5–8 cm) again, keeping them vertical all the time.

Repeat this gradual in-and-out movement of your palms, progressively decreasing the distance between the palms as you move them outward and go in again.

Your hands will become heavier, feel attracted like magnets, and be quite sticky as the aura energies of both hands merge.

You may notice a silvery white shimmer around each hand as it becomes progressively harder to separate them.

When your palms are no more than ¾ of an inch (2 cm) apart, lift your hands and arms over the center of your head to where you feel the outer limits of the aura. This outer edge of the newly cleansed and energized aura will be so sparkly and vibrating that it will be hard to miss.

Form a cup shape over your head with your hands, palms facing down and fingers together, around the outer aura edge.

Slowly follow the contours of the outer edge, letting each hand spontaneously move in unison down the sides of your body. You may encounter pressure, as though the outline of the aura is solidifying.

Stoop naturally, as though drawing an ellipse shape down each side of your body, still following the outermost aura limit with an invisible crayon, and end in front of your feet.

Finally, shake your fingers all around your head and shoulders, keeping the same arm-span distance, and you will see or sense silver sparks or stars outlining the aura.

Soft silver light will flow into the aura, all around your body—front, back, and from head to toe.

Finally, run your hands an extended arm span away down both sides of your body and then down the front, as though you were brushing off any excess aura energies with a hairbrush.

Bring these unseen aura energies down to the ground.

Then, briefly, hold your hands over a candle (not too close!) or in sunlight to cleanse them. You can do aura brushing any time during the day if someone has made you feel uncomfortable by getting too close to your aura space.

Either brush the unwanted aura energy to the ground, or roll it into an imaginary ball and drop it out of a window or even into a trash can. This is a way of symbolically removing unwanted energies from your space.

Write down your reflections after sealing your aura here. What have you learned about yourself and others after investigating auras?

_____

_____

_____

_____

_____

_____

_____

_____

_____

_____

_____

_____

_____

_____

_____

_____

_____

_____

_____

DATE   TIME

INTERACTION

OBSERVATIONS (SELF)

REACTIONS (OTHERS)

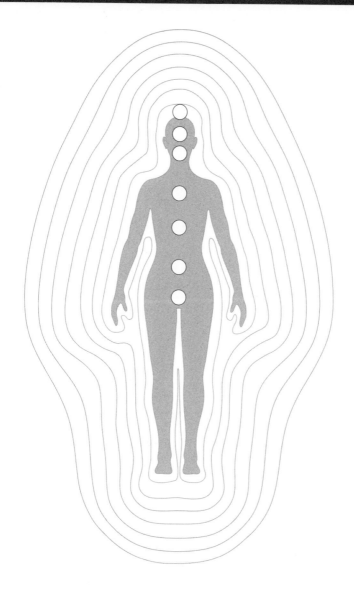

DATE _____ TIME _____

INTERACTION _____

_____

OBSERVATIONS (SELF) _____

_____

_____

_____

_____

_____

_____

_____

REACTIONS (OTHERS) _____

_____

_____

_____

_____

_____

_____

_____

_____

DATE   TIME

INTERACTION

OBSERVATIONS (SELF)

REACTIONS (OTHERS)

DATE   TIME

INTERACTION

OBSERVATIONS (SELF)

REACTIONS (OTHERS)

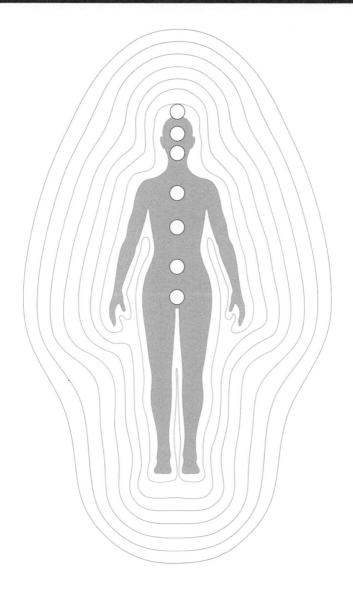

DATE   TIME

INTERACTION

OBSERVATIONS (SELF)

REACTIONS (OTHERS)

DATE   TIME

INTERACTION

OBSERVATIONS (SELF)

REACTIONS (OTHERS)

DATE   TIME

INTERACTION

OBSERVATIONS (SELF)

REACTIONS (OTHERS)

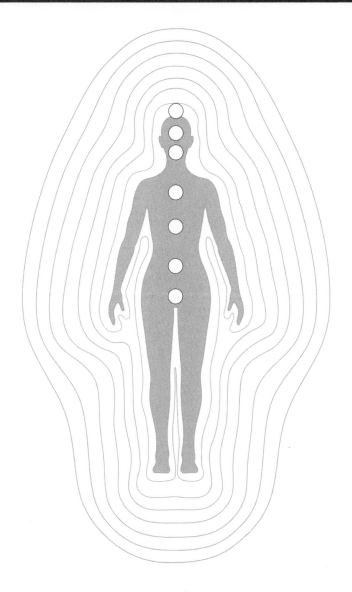

ABOUT THE AUTHOR

Cassandra Eason (Isle of Wight, England) is a best-selling author and a broadcaster on the paranormal. She has appeared many times on television and radio throughout the United States, Britain, Europe, and Australia. Cassandra originally trained as a teacher, and, while bringing up her five children, took a psychology honors degree with the intention of training as an educational psychologist.

A seemingly inexplicable psychic experience involving her two-year-old son Jack led to extensive research and the publication of a book on psychic children published by Random House in 1990. Since then, Cassandra has had more than 100 books published and translated into thirteen different languages. Cassandra also runs workshops in Australia and the United Kingdom and tours Australia each year. Many of her books have been serialized around the world and she has consulted with and contributed to such publications as the *UK Daily Mail*, *Daily Mirror*, *Daily Express*, *People*, *The Sun*, *News of the World* magazine, *Spirit and Destiny*, *Fate and Fortune*, *Prediction*, *Best and Bella*, *Homes and Gardens*, and *Good Housekeeping* and in *Woman's Day* and *New Idea* magazines in Australia. Cassandra now also regularly contributes to the UK magazine *Soul and Spirit*. She has long been acknowledged as a world expert on spellcraft and magick and has appeared many times on television and radio, including shows such as *Sky News*, ITV's *Strange but True*, BBC1's *Heaven and Earth*, and *Richard and Judy*, and she has also appeared in a series of mini films with Myleene Klass, and on Sky Living's *Jane Goldman Investigates*.